Flags **World**

 Libya

 Liechtenstein

 Lithuania

 Luxembourg

 Macedonia, FYRO

 Madagascar

 Malawi

 Malaysia

 Maldives

 Mali

 Malta

 Marshall Islands

 Mauritania

 Mauritius

 Mexico

 Micronesia

 Moldova

 Monaco

 Mongolia

 Montenegro

 Morocco

 Mozambique

 Myanmar

 Namibia

 Nauru

 Nepal

 Netherlands

New Zealand

 Nicaragua

 Niger

 Nigeria

Northern Marianas

North Korea

 Norway

 Oman

 Pakistan

 Palau

 Panama

 Papua New Guinea

Paraguay

Peru

 Philippines

 Poland

 Portugal

 Qatar

Romania

Russia

Rwanda

St. Kitts and Nevis

 St. Lucia

 St. Vincent & the Grenadines

 Samoa

San Marino

Sao Tomé and Pirncipe

Saudi Arabia

 Senegal

 Serbia

 Seychelles

Sierra Leone

Singapore

Slovakia

Slovenia

 Solomon Islands

 Somalia

South Africa

South Korea

Spain

Sri Lanka

Sudan

 Suriname

 Swaziland

Sweden

Switzerland

Syria

Taiwan

Tajikistan

 Tanzania

 Thailand

Togo

Tonga

 Trinidad and Tobago

Tunisia

Turkey

 Turkmenistan

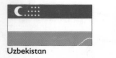 Tuvalu

 Uganda

Ukraine

United Arab Emirates

United Kingdom

United States of America

 Uruguay

Uzbekistan

 Vanuatu

Venezuela

 Vietnam

Yemen

Zambia

 Zimbabwe

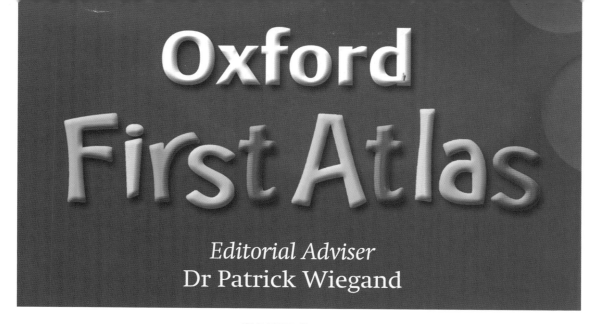

Oxford First Atlas

Editorial Adviser
Dr Patrick Wiegand

OXFORD
UNIVERSITY PRESS

Great Clarendon Street, Oxford OX2 6DP

Oxford University Press is a department of the University of Oxford.
It furthers the University's objective of excellence in research, scholarship,
and education by publishing worldwide in

Oxford   New York

Auckland   Cape Town   Dar es Salaam   Hong Kong   Karachi
Kuala Lumpur   Madrid   Melbourne   Mexico City   Nairobi
New Delhi   Shanghai   Taipei   Toronto

With offices in

Argentina   Austria   Brazil   Chile   Czech Republic   France   Greece
Guatemala   Hungary   Italy   Japan   Poland   Portugal   Singapore
South Korea   Switzerland   Thailand   Turkey   Ukraine   Vietnam

Oxford is a registered trade mark of Oxford University Press
in the UK and in certain other countries

© Oxford University Press 2010

First published 2010

© Maps copyright Oxford University Press

Cover illustrations by Mark Brierley

The moral rights of the authors have been asserted.

ISBN 978 0 19 830000 7 (hardback)
ISBN 978 0 19 830001 4 (paperback)

1 3 5 7 9 10 8 6 4 2

Printed in Singapore by KHL Printing Co. Pte Ltd.

Paper used in the production of this book is a natural, recyclable product made from wood grown in sustainable forests.
The manufacturing process conforms to the environmental regulations of the country of origin.

Acknowledgements

e publishers would like to thank the following for permission to reproduce photographs:
Planetary Visions Ltd/Science Photo Library, 4a Planet Observer/Science Photo Library, 8a David
ns/Alamy, 8b Design Pics Inc/Rex Features, 8c John Warburton-Lee/Photolibrary.com, 8d Christopher
ell/Shutterstock.com, 10a Gary Brown/Rex Features, 10b Arco Images GmbH/Alamy, 10c Micha
litzki/Corbis, 10d Des Willie/Alamy, 10e SGM SGM/Photolibrary.com, 12a Alan Copson/
tolibrary.com, 12b OUP/Corel, 12c Simon Batley/Alamy, 12d Geoff A Howard/Alamy, 13a Alinari/Rex
tures, 16a John Frumm/Photolibrary.com, 16b Sue Flood/Getty Images, 16c John Henry Claude Wilson/
tolibrary.com, 17a Alexandra Winkler/Reuters/Corbis, 18a Leonid Shcheglov/Shutterstock.com, 18b Joe
Alamy,18c Charles Stirling/Alamy, 18d Britain on View/ Photolibrary.com, 18e OUP/Corel, 20a Arco
ges GmbH/Alamy, 20b Marianna Sulic/Getty Images, 20c Hashim Pudiyapura/Shutterstock.com, 20d
1 Banton/Shutterstock.com, 21a Juan Carlos Munoz/Photolibrary.com, 21b Corbis/Photolibrary.com, 21c
odboard/Photolibrary.com, 22a Joe McDonald/Corbis, 22b Rafael Ramirez Lee/Shutterstock.com, 23a Jan
twald/Shutterstock.com, 23b OUP/Corbis, 24a Getmapping PLC/Science Photo Library, 26a Gavin
lier/Getty Images, 26b Reuters/Corbis, 26c Sarah Leen/Getty Images, 27a Ted Mead/Photolibrary.com,
28a Chris Warren/ Photolibrary of Wales, 28b Amra Pasic/Shutterstock.com, 28c Rex Butcher/Getty Images,
28d Ken McKay/Rex Features, 28e Phil Noble/Reuters/Corbis, 28f Rod Edwards/Photolibrary.com, 30a
Feraru Nicolae/Shutterstock.com, 30b OUP/Corbis, 30c Wong Tsu Shi/Shutterstock.com, 30d Pborowka/
Shutterstock.com, 31a Craig Hanson/Shutterstock.com, 31b TOSP Photo/Shutterstock.com, 35a Siepmann
Siepmann/Photolibrary.com, 35b prism68/Shutterstock.com, 37a Rex/Rex Features, 37b Dahlquist
Ron/Photolibrary.com, 39a Joshua Haviv/Shutterstock.com, 39b Graça Victoria/ Shutterstock.com, 39c
OUP/Photodisc, 39d Andre Jenny/Alamy, 41a JTB Photo Communications, Inc./Alamy, 41b Paul
Souders/Getty Images, 41c Yoshio Tomii Photo Studio/Photolibrary.com, 41d Tom C Amon/
Shutterstock.com, 43a Alan Ward/Shutterstock.com, 43b OUP/Digital Vision, 43c Neil Cooper/Alamy, 43d
David C Poole/Photolibrary.com, 45a Purestock/Photolibrary.com, 45b OUP/Photodisc, 45c Jeff Hunter/Getty
Images, 45d Steve Wisbauer/Getty Images, 46a Bryan & Cherry Alexander Photography/Alamy, 47a
blickwinkel/Alamy

Illustrations by: Mark Brierley

2 Contents

© Oxford University Press

The Earth is a planet in space. It is a sphere.

If you look at the Earth from space you can see land, sea and clouds. You cannot see countries. To see countries you need a map.

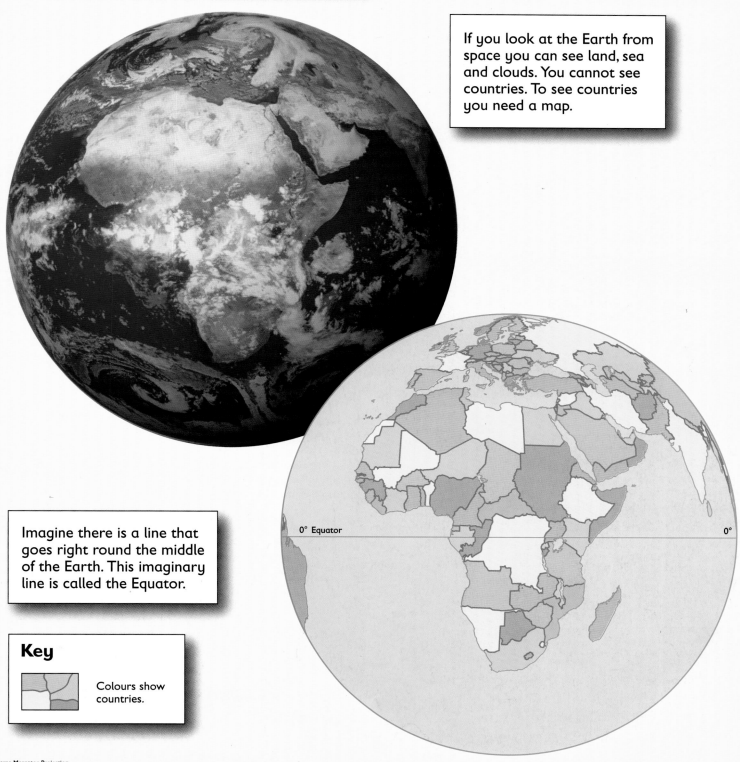

Imagine there is a line that goes right round the middle of the Earth. This imaginary line is called the Equator.

0° Equator   0°

Key

Colours show countries.

Transverse Mercator Projection
© Oxford University Press

4 The British Isles

Great Britain and Ireland are islands. They are land with sea all around. These two large islands, together with many smaller ones, make up the British Isles.

This is a picture of the British Isles from space.

This is a map of the British Isles.

Ireland

Isle of Man

Great Britain

Channel Islands

There are two countries in the British Isles. The key shows what the colours and symbols on the map stand for.

The British Isles are small compared to many places in the world. Can you find the British Isles on a globe?

Key

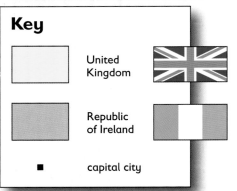

United Kingdom

Republic of Ireland

■ capital city

Dublin ■
Republic of Ireland

United Kingdom

London ■

The United Kingdom

England, Scotland and Wales together with Northern Ireland make the **United Kingdom**.

Key

England

Scotland

Wales

Northern Ireland

■ capital city

Flags

England

Scotland

Wales

Northern Ireland

Scotland

Edinburgh

Northern
Ireland
Belfast

REPUBLIC
OF IRELAND

UNITED
KINGDOM

England

Wales

Cardiff

London ■

FRANCE

A capital city is the most important city in a country. It is where the government meets. The capital city of the United Kingdom is London.

Transverse Mercator Projection
© Oxford University Press

6 Countries of the world

A country is a land with its own people and its own laws.

Key

Colours show countries.

Some countries are too small to be named on this map.

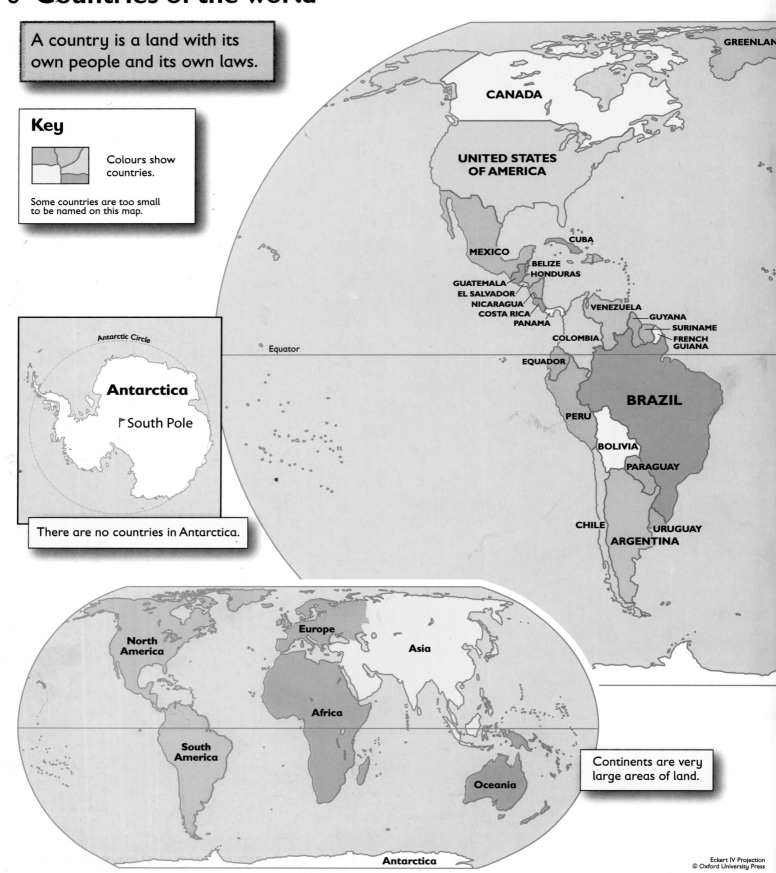

Antarctica

⌐South Pole

Antarctic Circle

There are no countries in Antarctica.

GREENLAN

CANADA

UNITED STATES OF AMERICA

CUBA

MEXICO

BELIZE
HONDURAS
GUATEMALA
EL SALVADOR
NICARAGUA
COSTA RICA
PANAMA

VENEZUELA

GUYANA
SURINAME
FRENCH GUIANA

COLOMBIA

Equator

EQUADOR

BRAZIL

PERU

BOLIVIA

PARAGUAY

CHILE

URUGUAY

ARGENTINA

North America

Europe

Asia

Africa

South America

Oceania

Antarctica

Continents are very large areas of land.

Eckert IV Projection
© Oxford University Press

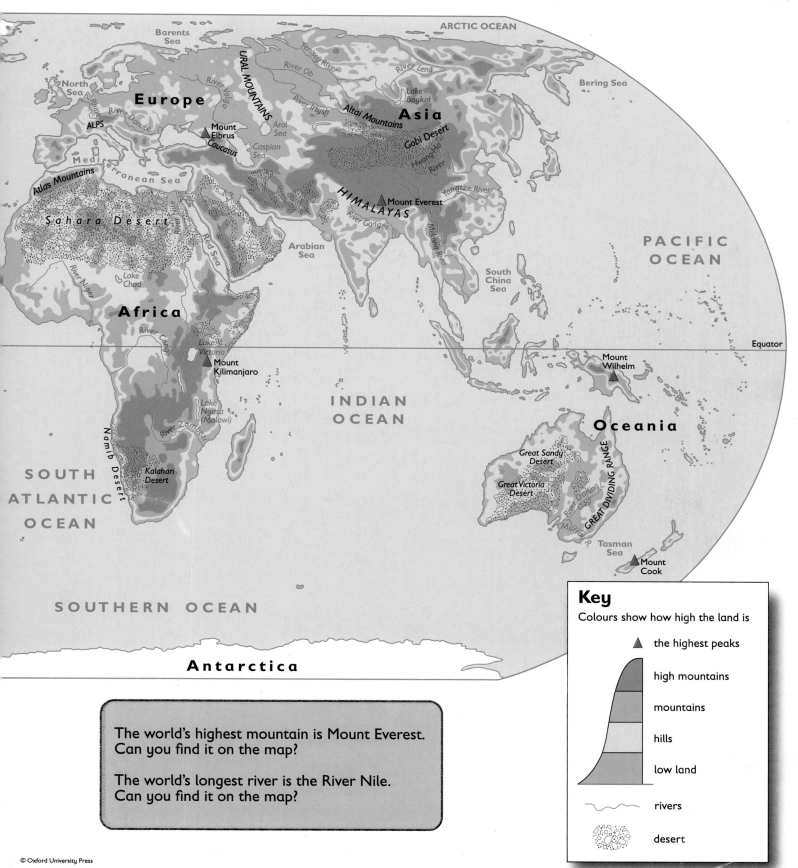

ARCTIC OCEAN

Barents
Sea

North
Sea

Europe

ALPS

Mediterranean Sea

Atlas Mountains

Sahara Desert

River Niger

Lake
Chad

Africa

River Congo

Lake
Victoria

▲ Mount
Kilimanjaro

Lake
Nyasa
(Malawi)

River Zambezi

Namib Desert

Kalahari
Desert

**SOUTH
ATLANTIC
OCEAN**

URAL MOUNTAINS

River Volga

River Danube

▲ Mount
Elbrus
Caucasus

Aral
Sea

Caspian
Sea

River Nile

Red Sea

Arabian
Sea

River Ob

Yenisey River

River Irtysh

Altai Mountains

Lake
Baykal

River Lena

Asia

Gobi Desert

Hwang Ho
River

HIMALAYAS ▲ Mount Everest

River Ganges

Yangtze River

Mekong River

South
China
Sea

Bering Sea

**PACIFIC
OCEAN**

Equator

▲ Mount
Wilhelm

Oceania

Great Sandy
Desert

Great Victoria
Desert

River Darling

GREAT DIVIDING RANGE

Murray R

Tasman
Sea

▲ Mount
Cook

**INDIAN
OCEAN**

SOUTHERN OCEAN

Antarctica

The world's highest mountain is Mount Everest.
Can you find it on the map?

The world's longest river is the River Nile.
Can you find it on the map?

Key

Colours show how high the land is

▲ the highest peaks

high mountains

mountains

hills

low land

~~~ rivers

⋯ desert

12 By the sea

Where the land meets the sea is called the **coast**.

beach

A beach is land by the edge of the sea that is covered with sand or small stones.

cliff

A cliff is a hill with one side that goes straight down to the sea.

port

A port is a place on the coast where ships come and go.

seaside resort

A seaside resort is a place where you go for a seaside holiday.

By the sea in the United Kingdom

Key

	sandy beaches
	cliffs
⚓	port
⛱	seaside resort
〰	river

ATLANTIC OCEAN

Scotland

Northern Ireland

North Sea

River Spey

River Dee

Forth

River Clyde

River Tweed

Stranraer

Tyne

River Tyne

Belfast

Tees and Hartlepool

Whitby

Scarborough

Heysham

Bridlington

Blackpool

Irish Sea

Hull

River Aire

Llandudno

Liverpool

Holyhead

England

Grimsby and Illingham

Skegness

River Trent

River Severn

Great Yarmouth

Wales

River Wye

River Avon

River Great Ouse

Felixstowe

Milford Haven

River Thames

Southend-on-Sea

Ilfracombe

London

Dover

Southampton

Portsmouth

Brighton

Weymouth

Newhaven

Eastbourne

St. Ives

Torquay

Plymouth

English Channel

What was the seaside like in the past?
How does the seaside look
different today?

Transverse Mercator Projection
© Oxford University Press

14 Our weather

The weather is how it is outside, for example, whether it is hot or cold, sunny or raining.

spring			summer			autumn			winter		
March	April	May	June	July	August	September	October	November	December	January	February

The year has twelve months and four seasons.

Our summers are usually warm or hot.
Our winters are usually cool or cold.

The weather is slightly different from place to place in the British Isles.

The **north** has more cold days.

north

west

east

south

The **west** has more rainy days.

The **east** has more dry, sunny days.

The **south** has more warm days.

Key

	places with warm summer days and cold winter days
	places with hot summer days and cool winter days
☁	places with a lot of rain
☃	places with a lot of snow in winter

north

west — **east**

south

ATLANTIC OCEAN

North Sea

Braemar

UNITED KINGDOM

Sprinkling Tarn

REPUBLIC OF IRELAND

Irish Sea

St. Osyth

Isles of Scilly

English Channel

FRANCE

The warmest place in Britain is the Isles of Scilly.

The coldest place in Britain is Braemar.

The wettest place in Britain is Sprinkling Tarn.

The driest place in Britain is St. Osyth.

Can you find these places on the map?

Transverse Mercator Projection
© Oxford University Press

16 Weather around the world

Homes and clothes around the world are designed according to what the weather is usually like.

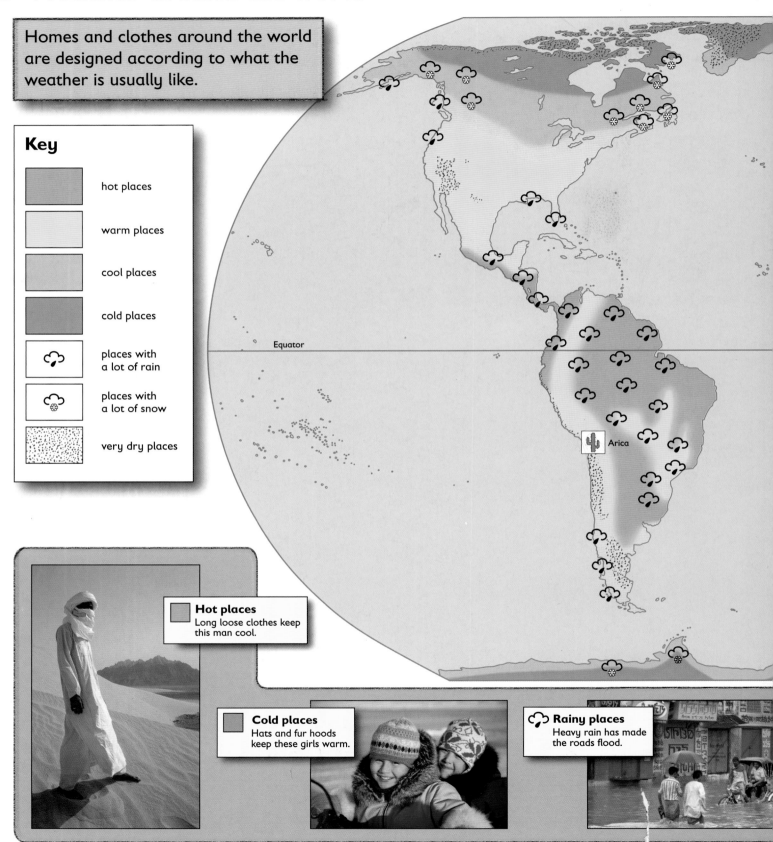

Key

- hot places
- warm places
- cool places
- cold places
- places with a lot of rain
- places with a lot of snow
- very dry places

Equator

Arica

Hot places
Long loose clothes keep this man cool.

Cold places
Hats and fur hoods keep these girls warm.

Rainy places
Heavy rain has made the roads flood.

Eckert IV Projection
© Oxford University Press

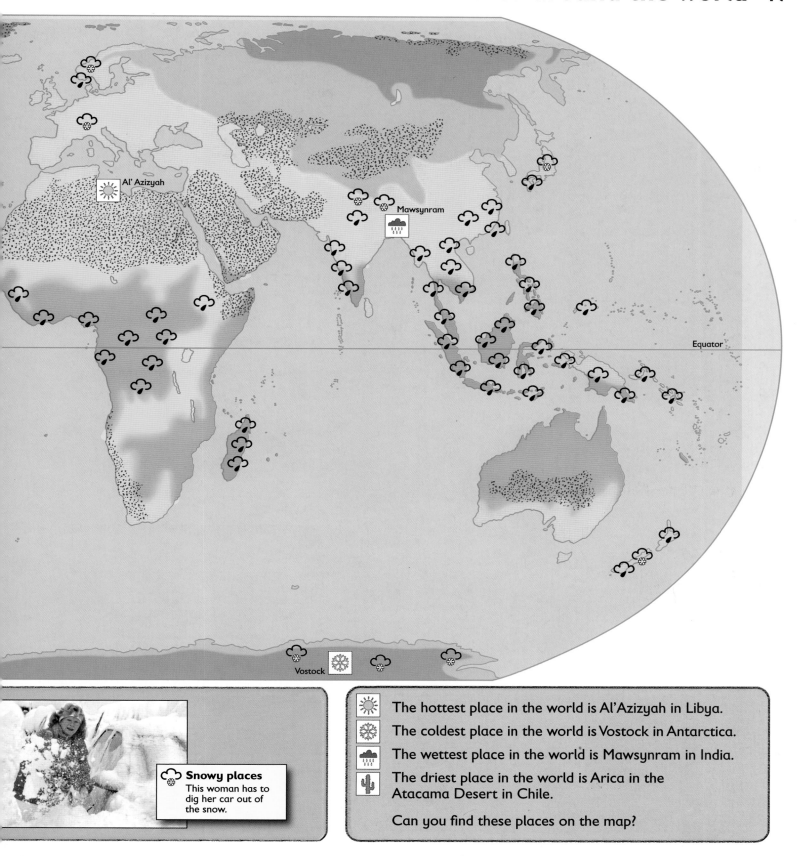

Al' Azizyah

Mawsynram

Equator

Vostock

Snowy places
This woman has to dig her car out of the snow.

The hottest place in the world is Al'Azizyah in Libya.

The coldest place in the world is Vostock in Antarctica.

The wettest place in the world is Mawsynram in India.

The driest place in the world is Arica in the Atacama Desert in Chile.

Can you find these places on the map?

18 Our environment

The environment is the air, land and water that surrounds us. We need to protect the environment.

farmland

Farmers use the land to produce food by growing crops and keeping animals.

forest and woodland

Land used to grow trees for wood.

built-up areas

Land with houses, shops, factories and other buildings.

National Parks

Beautiful countryside that is specially protected.

Heritage Coast

Beautiful coastal scenery that is specially protected.

Environments in the United Kingdom

Key

	farmland
🌲	forest and woodland
	built-up areas
	National Parks
	Heritage Coast

ATLANTIC OCEAN

Scotland

Cairngorms
The Trossachs
Loch Lomond
Aberdeen
Dundee
Glasgow
Edinburgh

North Sea

Northern Ireland

Belfast

Northumberland
Newcastle upon Tyne
Middlesbrough

Irish Sea

Lake District
North York Moors
Yorkshire Dales
Leeds
Kingston upon Hull
Manchester
Liverpool
Sheffield
Peak District

Snowdonia

The Broads
Birmingham
Leicester
Norwich

Wales

Pembrokeshire Coast
Brecon Beacons
Cardiff

England

Bristol
London

Exmoor
New Forest
Southampton
South Downs

Dartmoor

English Channel

Most National Parks have hills or mountains.

Which is the nearest National Park to where you live?

Transverse Mercator Projection
© Oxford University Press

20 Environments around the world

There are different environments around the world. In some places there are very many plants, in others very few.

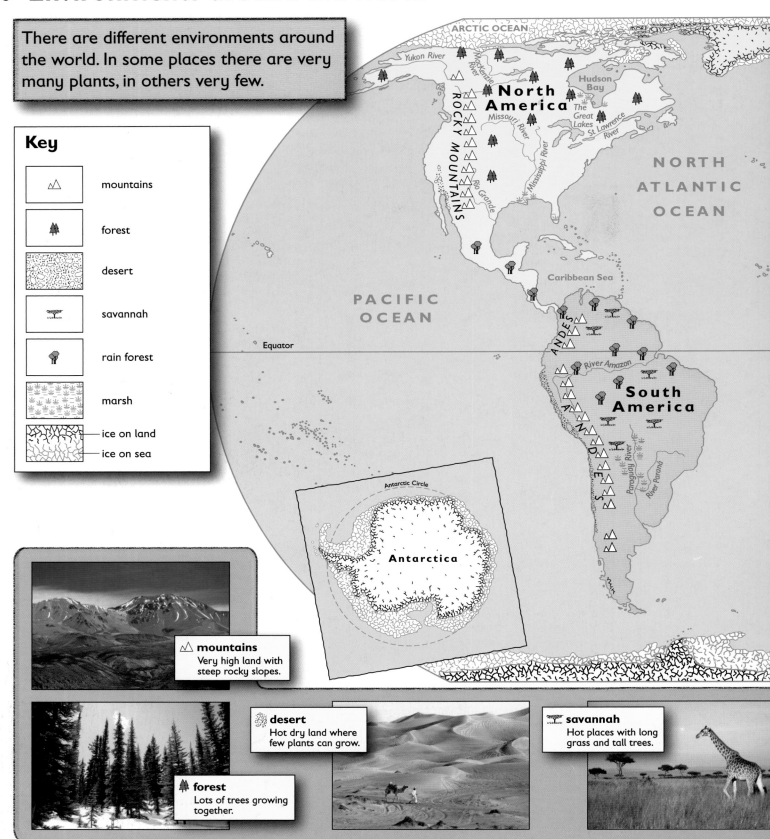

Key

△	mountains
🌲	forest
▨	desert
🌴	savannah
🌳	rain forest
⁂	marsh
❅	ice on land
	ice on sea

△ mountains
Very high land with steep rocky slopes.

🌲 forest
Lots of trees growing together.

🌵 desert
Hot dry land where few plants can grow.

🌴 savannah
Hot places with long grass and tall trees.

Eckert IV Projection
© Oxford University Press

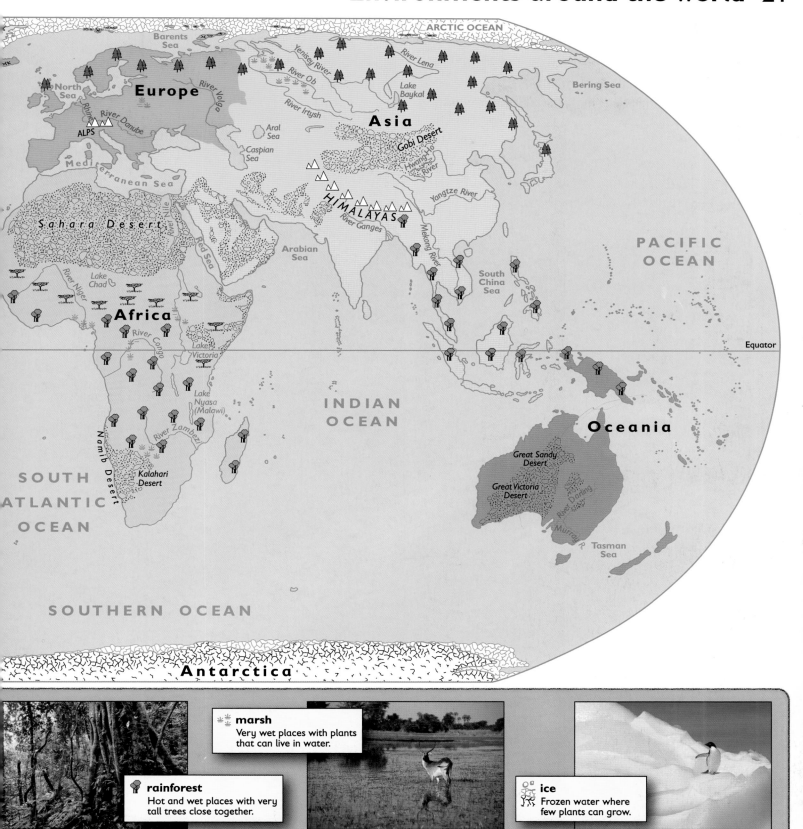

ARCTIC OCEAN

Barents Sea

North Sea

Europe

River Volga

River Danube

Rhine

ALPS

Mediterranean Sea

Yenisey River

River Ob

River Irtysh

Aral Sea

Caspian Sea

Asia

Lake Baykal

River Lena

Bering Sea

Gobi Desert

Hwang Ho River

HIMALAYAS

River Ganges

Yangtze River

Mekong River

South China Sea

PACIFIC OCEAN

Sahara Desert

River Nile

Red Sea

Arabian Sea

River Niger

Lake Chad

Africa

River Congo

Lake Victoria

Lake Nyasa (Malawi)

River Zambezi

Namib Desert

Kalahari Desert

INDIAN OCEAN

Equator

Oceania

Great Sandy Desert

Great Victoria Desert

River Darling

Murray R.

Tasman Sea

SOUTH ATLANTIC OCEAN

SOUTHERN OCEAN

Antarctica

🌿 **marsh**
Very wet places with plants that can live in water.

🌳 **rainforest**
Hot and wet places with very tall trees close together.

❄ **ice**
Frozen water where few plants can grow.

22 Animals around the world

Each of these animals is suited to the environment in which it lives. If the environment changes, animals may die.

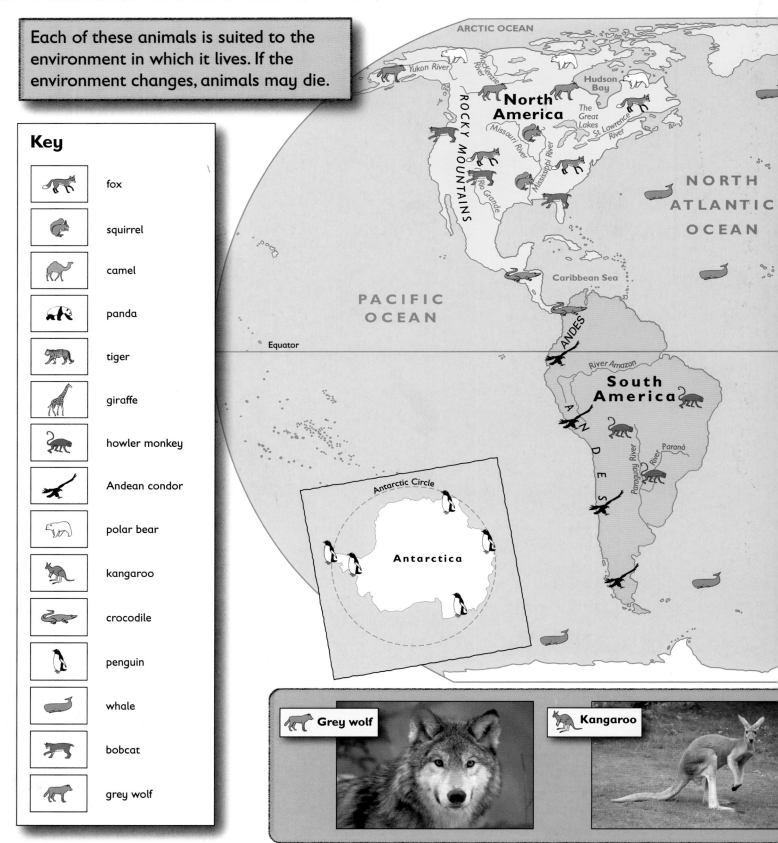

Key

- fox
- squirrel
- camel
- panda
- tiger
- giraffe
- howler monkey
- Andean condor
- polar bear
- kangaroo
- crocodile
- penguin
- whale
- bobcat
- grey wolf

Grey wolf

Kangaroo

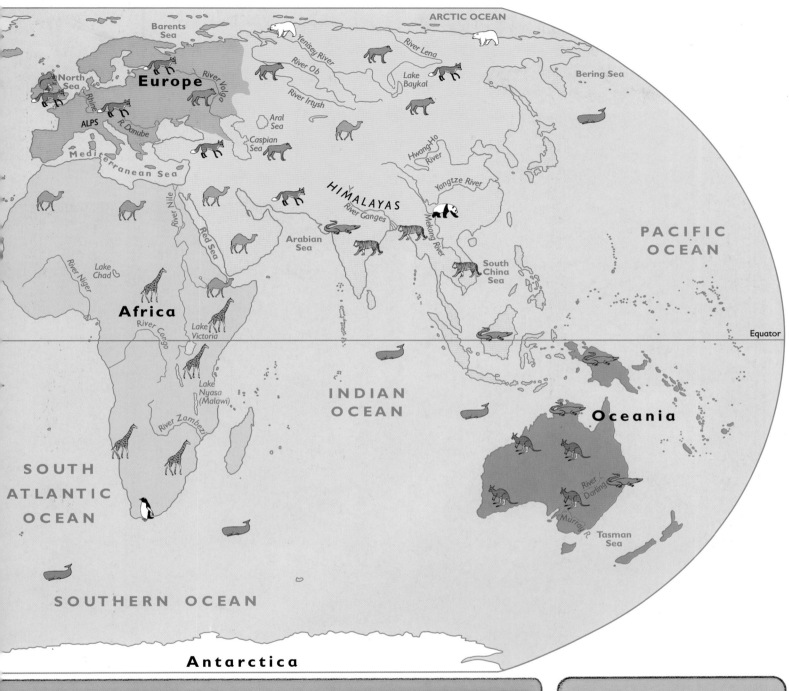

Panda

Tiger

Choose an animal from each continent.

Can you say why it is especially suited to its environment?

24 Towns and cities

A town is a place with a lot of houses, shops, factories, offices and other buildings. A city is a very large town. Towns and cities are built-up areas.

built-up area

This photograph shows part of Birmingham seen from the air. Can you find:

- A street with houses
- A football stadium
- A main road
- A park
- A carpark
- A railway line

Towns and cities in the United Kingdom

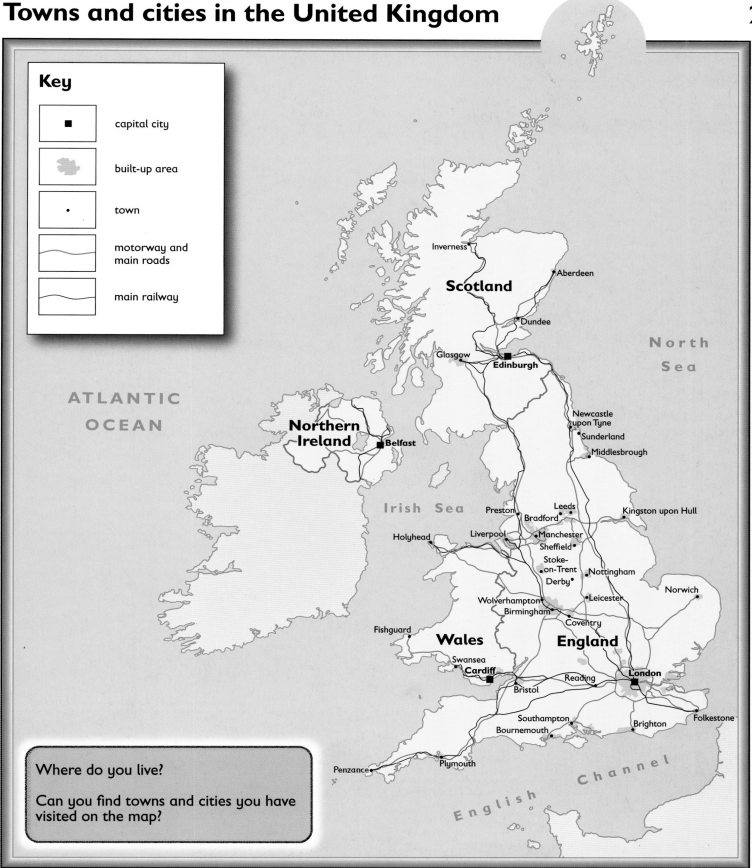

Key

- ■ capital city
- built-up area
- • town
- motorway and main roads
- main railway

ATLANTIC OCEAN

Inverness

Aberdeen

Scotland

Dundee

Glasgow
Edinburgh

North Sea

Newcastle upon Tyne

Sunderland

Middlesbrough

Northern Ireland

Belfast

Irish Sea

Preston

Leeds

Bradford

Kingston upon Hull

Holyhead

Liverpool

Manchester

Sheffield

Stoke-on-Trent

Nottingham

Derby

Norwich

Leicester

Wolverhampton

Birmingham

Coventry

Fishguard

Wales

England

Swansea

Cardiff

Reading

London

Bristol

Southampton

Brighton

Folkestone

Bournemouth

Penzance

Plymouth

English Channel

Where do you live?

Can you find towns and cities you have visited on the map?

Transverse Mercator Projection
© Oxford University Press

Some places in the world are very crowded. Other places have very few people.

Key

- one million people live near each dot
- ⊙ the world's largest cities

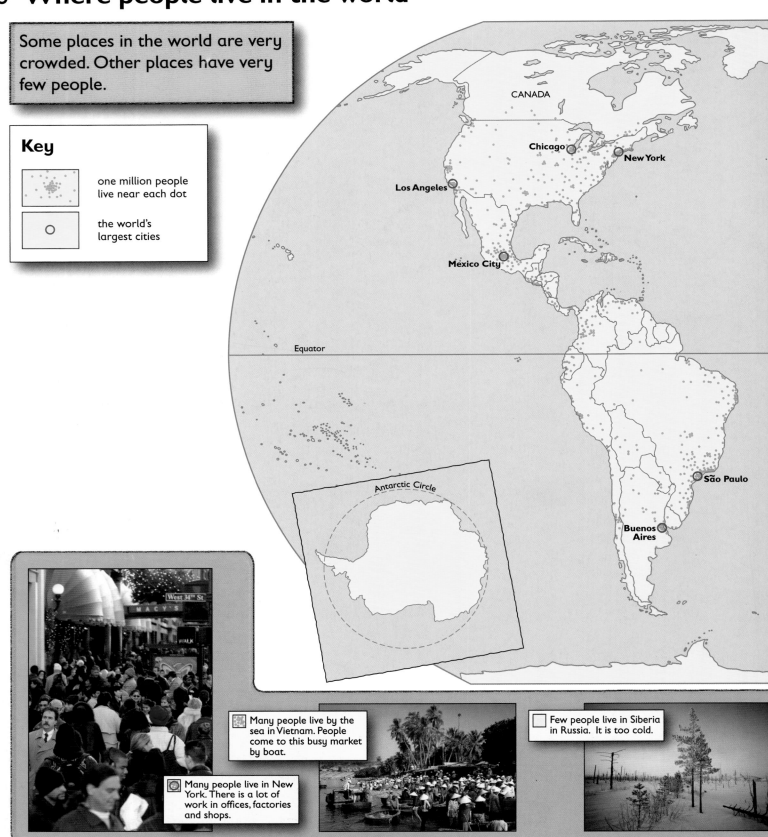

CANADA

Chicago
New York
Los Angeles
Mexico City

Equator

Antarctic Circle

São Paulo

Buenos Aires

West 34ᵀᴴ St

Many people live in New York. There is a lot of work in offices, factories and shops.

Many people live by the sea in Vietnam. People come to this busy market by boat.

Few people live in Siberia in Russia. It is too cold.

Eckert IV Projection
© Oxford University Press

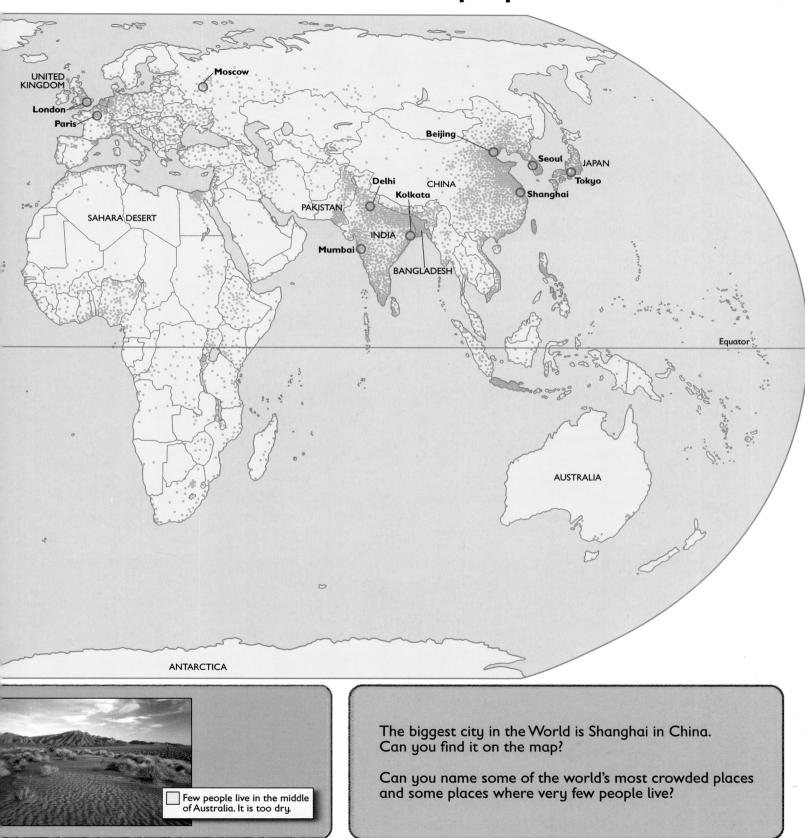

UNITED
KINGDOM
Moscow
London
Paris
Beijing
Seoul   JAPAN
Delhi   Tokyo
CHINA   Shanghai
PAKISTAN   Kolkata
INDIA
Mumbai
BANGLADESH
SAHARA DESERT
AUSTRALIA
Equator
ANTARCTICA

Few people live in the middle
of Australia. It is too dry.

The biggest city in the World is Shanghai in China.
Can you find it on the map?

Can you name some of the world's most crowded places
and some places where very few people live?

Holidays are time off from school or work. What is there to see and do near where you live?

Castles are large strong buildings with thick stone walls and tall towers. They were built long ago to keep people safe from their enemies.

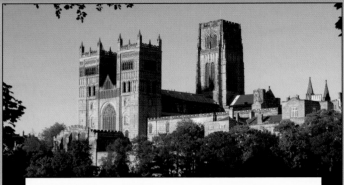

Cathedrals are big churches that were built by Christians to worship God.

Museums are places where interesting things are kept for people to go and see.

Theme parks are very large outdoor play areas with exciting rides.

Zoos are places where wild animals are kept so that people can go and see them up close.

Some parts of the **countryside and coast** are especially beautiful and many people go on holiday to enjoy the views.

Key

castle	
cathedral	
museum	
theme park	
zoo	
countryside and coast	
built-up area	

North Sea

Scotland

Edinburgh Castle

National Museum of Scotland, Edinburgh

Kelvingrove Art Gallery and Museum, Glasgow

Edinburgh Zoo

Giant's Causeway

Northern Ireland

Belfast Zoo

ATLANTIC OCEAN

Lake District

Durham Cathedral

North York Moors

Flamingoland

Irish Sea

Blackpool Pleasure Beach

Conwy Castle

Peak District

Chester Zoo

Caernarfon Castle

Alton Towers

The Broads

England

Drayton Manor

Pembrokeshire Coast

Wales

Warwick Castle

St. David's Cathedral

Big Pit, National Coal Museum

Windsor Castle

Canterbury Cathedral

Cardiff Castle

Salisbury Cathedral

Thorpe Park

Jurassic Coast

English Channel

Inner London

British Museum

London Zoo

St. Paul's Cathedral

Science Museum

Tower of London

Natural History Museum

Victoria & Albert Museum

Westminster Abbey

Transverse Mercator Projection
© Oxford University Press

A passport is a booklet that shows who you are and what country you come from. You need a passport to travel to other countries. Here are some places in the world you might like to visit.

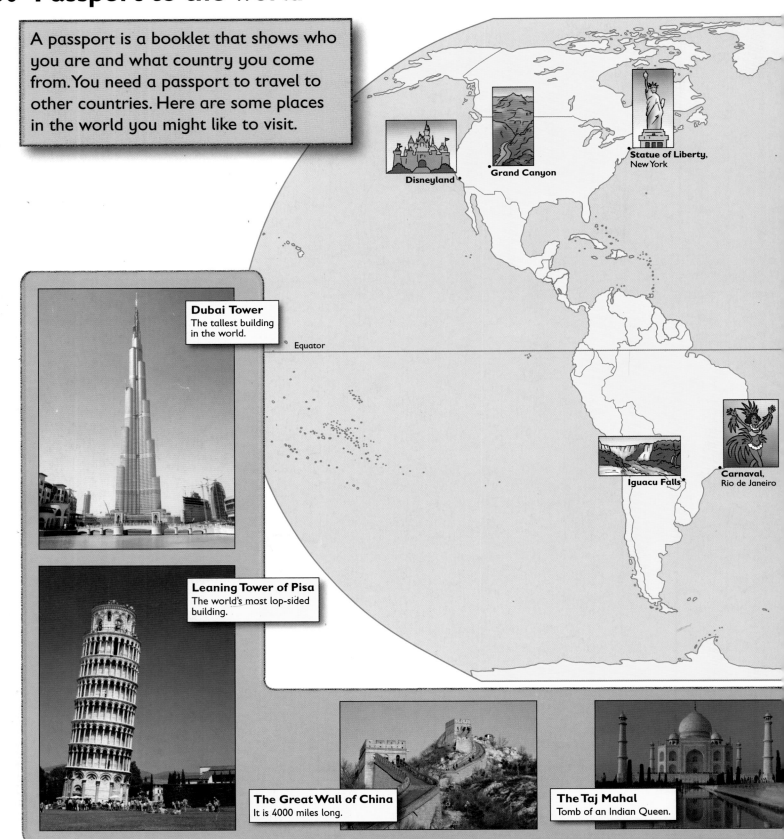

Disneyland

Grand Canyon

Statue of Liberty, New York

Equator

Iguacu Falls

Carnaval, Rio de Janeiro

Dubai Tower
The tallest building in the world.

Leaning Tower of Pisa
The world's most lop-sided building.

The Great Wall of China
It is 4000 miles long.

The Taj Mahal
Tomb of an Indian Queen.

Eckert IV Projection
© Oxford University Press

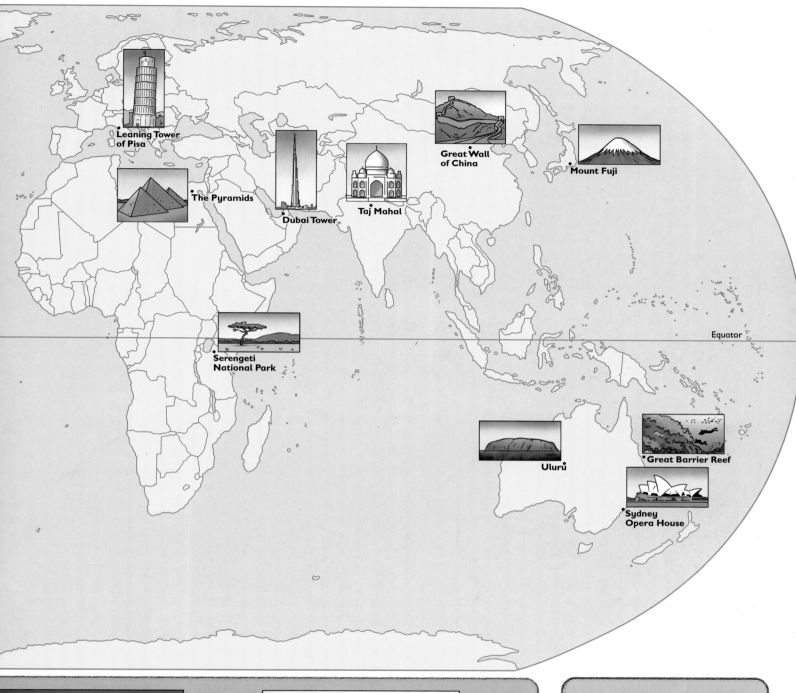

Leaning Tower of Pisa

The Pyramids

Dubai Tower

Taj Mahal

Great Wall of China

Mount Fuji

Serengeti National Park

Equator

Uluru

Great Barrier Reef

Sydney Opera House

Mount Fuji
A volcano covered in snow.

The Grand Canyon
It is more than a mile deep.

Where in the world would you like to go?

How will you get there?

What will it be like when you are there?

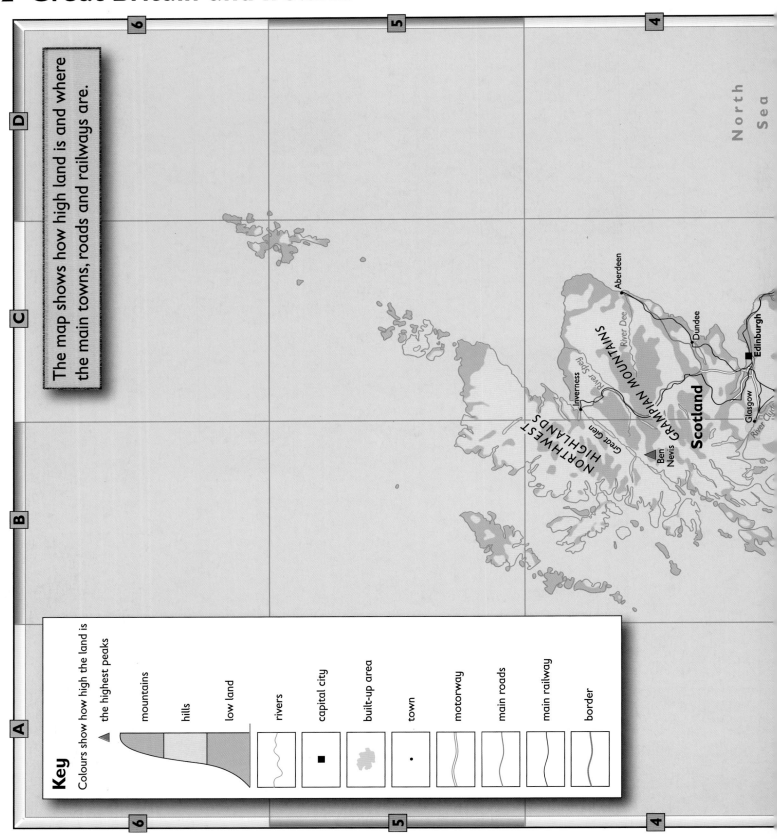

The map shows how high high land is and where the main towns, roads and railways are.

Key

Colours show how high the land is

▲ the highest peaks

- mountains
- hills
- low land

- rivers
- capital city ■
- built-up area
- town ·
- motorway
- main roads
- main railway
- border

North Sea

Aberdeen
Dundee
Edinburgh
Inverness
River Spey
River Dee
NORTHWEST HIGHLANDS
GRAMPIAN MOUNTAINS
Great Glen
Ben Nevis
Scotland
Glasgow
River Clyde

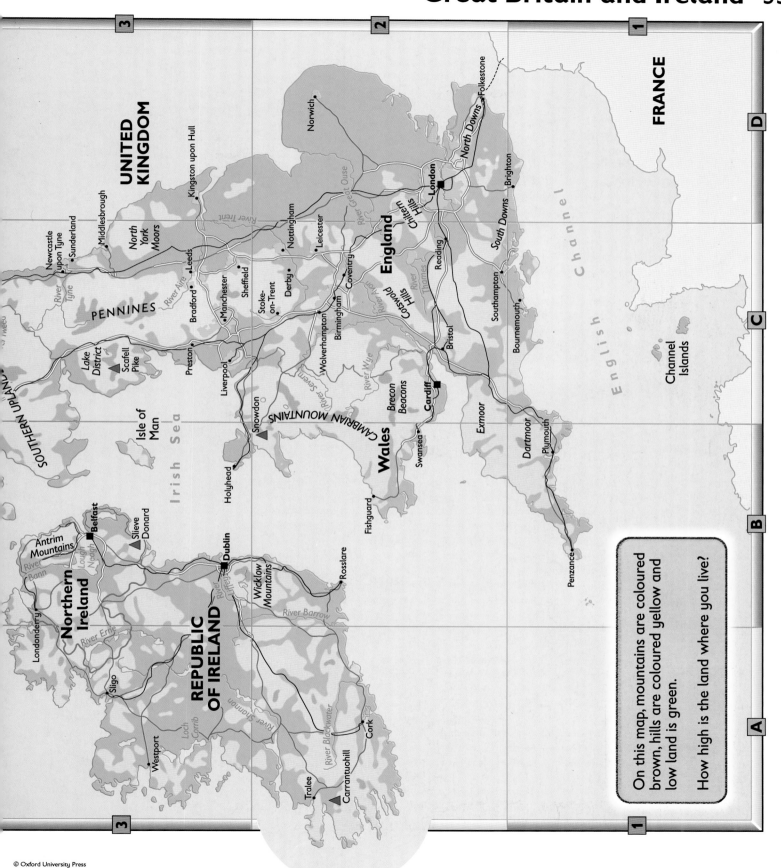

On this map, mountains are coloured brown, hills are coloured yellow and low land is green.

How high is the land where you live?

FRANCE

UNITED KINGDOM

England

Wales

Northern Ireland

REPUBLIC OF IRELAND

PENNINES

SOUTHERN UPLANDS

CAMBRIAN MOUNTAINS

Cotswold Hills

Chiltern Hills

North Downs

South Downs

North York Moors

Lake District

Scafell Pike

Snowdon

Brecon Beacons

Exmoor

Dartmoor

Antrim Mountains

Slieve Donard

Wicklow Mountains

Carrantuohill

Isle of Man

Irish Sea

English Channel

Channel Islands

Newcastle upon Tyne
Sunderland
Middlesbrough
Kingston upon Hull
Leeds
Bradford
Manchester
Sheffield
Stoke-on-Trent
Derby
Nottingham
Leicester
Coventry
Birmingham
Wolverhampton
Norwich
Reading
London
Folkestone
Brighton
Southampton
Bournemouth
Bristol
Cardiff
Swansea
Fishguard
Plymouth
Penzance
Preston
Liverpool
Holyhead
Belfast
Londonderry
Sligo
Westport
Dublin
Rosslare
Cork
Tralee

River Tyne
River Tweed
River Aire
River Trent
Great Ouse
River Thames
River Avon
River Severn
River Wye
River Bann
River Erne
River Liffey
River Barrow
River Shannon
River Blackwater
Lough Neagh
Lough Corrib

© Oxford University Press

ICELAND
Reykjavik

SWEDEN
FINLAND

NORWAY
Oslo
Stockholm
Helsinki
St. Petersburg

North
Sea

DENMARK
Copenhagen
Tallinn
ESTONIA

Riga
LATVIA

UNITED
KINGDOM
LITHUANIA
Vilnius

REPUBLIC
OF IRELAND
Dublin
Minsk

NETHERLANDS
Amsterdam
Berlin
POLAND
BELARUS

London
Brussels
BELGIUM
River Rhine
GERMANY
Warsaw

LUXEMBOURG
Prague
CZECH
REPUBLIC
UKRAINE

River Seine
Paris
Vienna
River Danube
SLOVAKIA
Bratislava

FRANCE
Bern
SWITZERLAND
AUSTRIA
Budapest
HUNGARY
Chisinău
MOLDOVA

ATLANTIC
OCEAN
Mont
Blanc
Alps
Ljubljana
SLOVENIA
Zagreb
CROATIA
ROMANIA
Bucharest

Pyrenées
BOSNIA-
HERZEGOVINA
Belgrade

Corsica
ITALY
Sarajevo
MONTENEGRO
SERBIA
BULGARIA

PORTUGAL
Madrid
SPAIN
Sardinia
Rome
Podgorica
KOSOVO
Sofia
MACEDONIA
Skopje
Istanbul

Majorca
Tiranë
ALBANIA

Lisbon
GREECE

Sicily
Athens

MALTA
Mediterranean Sea
Crete

Modified Gall Projection
© Oxford University Press

Key

▦	Colours show countries
■	capital cities
•	other cities
▲	highest peaks
⌂	mountains
🌲	cold forest
▦	marsh

RUSSIA

River Volga

Moscow

Kiev

Black Sea

Mount Elbrus

Caucasus

GEORGIA

Tbilisi

Ankara

TURKEY

CYPRUS

There are many European languages.

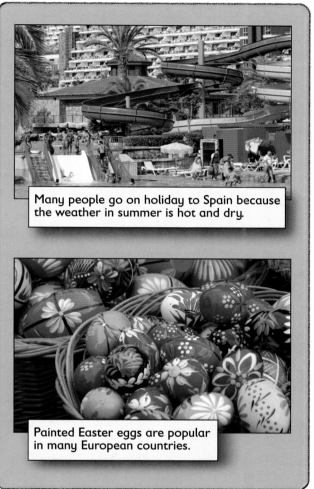

Many people go on holiday to Spain because the weather in summer is hot and dry.

Painted Easter eggs are popular in many European countries.

Do you know what language people speak in each of these countries?

France
Spain
Greece
Italy
The Netherlands

36 Asia

A   B   C

RUSSIA

Yenisey River

River Ob

River Lena

River Volga

Moscow

KAZAKHSTAN

Astana

River Irtysh

Altai Mountains

Ulan Bator

MONGOLIA

ARMENIA

Yerevan

Baku

Caspian Sea

AZERBAIJAN

UZBEKISTAN

Tashkent

Bishkek

KYRGYZSTAN

Gobi Desert

Beijing

NORTH KOREA

Pyongyang

TURKMENISTAN

Ashgabat

TAJIKISTAN

Dushanbe

Mount K2

CHINA

Hwang-Ho River

Seoul

SOUTH KOREA

Tehran

AFGHANISTAN

Kabul

SYRIA

Beirut

Damascus

Baghdad

LEBANON

ISRAEL

Jerusalem

Amman

JORDAN

IRAQ

IRAN

Islamabad

Himalayas

Mekong River

Shanghai

New Delhi

NEPAL

Mount Everest

Kathmandu

Thimphu

BHUTAN

Yangtze River

Kuwait

KUWAIT

Kuwait City

PAKISTAN

River Ganges

Taipei

QATAR

Riyadh

UNITED ARAB EMIRATES

Muscat

BANGLADESH

Dhaka

Kolkata

TAIWAN

SAUDI ARABIA

OMAN

INDIA

Mumbai

MYANMAR

Hanoi

Hong Kong

LAOS

Vientiane

Yangon

YEMEN

Sana

THAILAND

Bangkok

Manila

PHILIPPINES

CAMBODIA

VIETNAM

Phnom Penh

Colombo

SRI LANKA

MALAYSIA

BRUNEI

Bandar Seri Begawan

Kuala Lumpur

SINGAPORE

INDONESIA

Jakarta

Dili

EAST TIMOR

INDIAN OCEAN

How big is Asia?

Compare with the British Isles.

A   B   C

Modified Gall Projection
© Oxford University Press

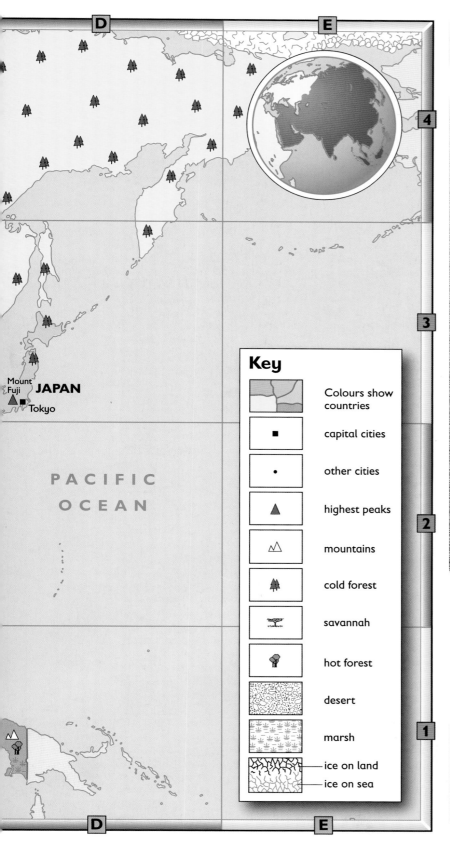

Mount Fuji
JAPAN
Tokyo

PACIFIC OCEAN

Key

	Colours show countries
■	capital cities
•	other cities
▲	highest peaks
⋀⋀	mountains
🌲	cold forest
	savannah
	hot forest
	desert
	marsh
	ice on land
	ice on sea

Asia is the largest continent.

It takes a whole week to travel across Russia by train.

In China and Japan people eat with chopsticks.

Russia is the largest country in the world. Can you find Russia on the map?

China has more people than any other country. Can you find China on the map?

38 North America

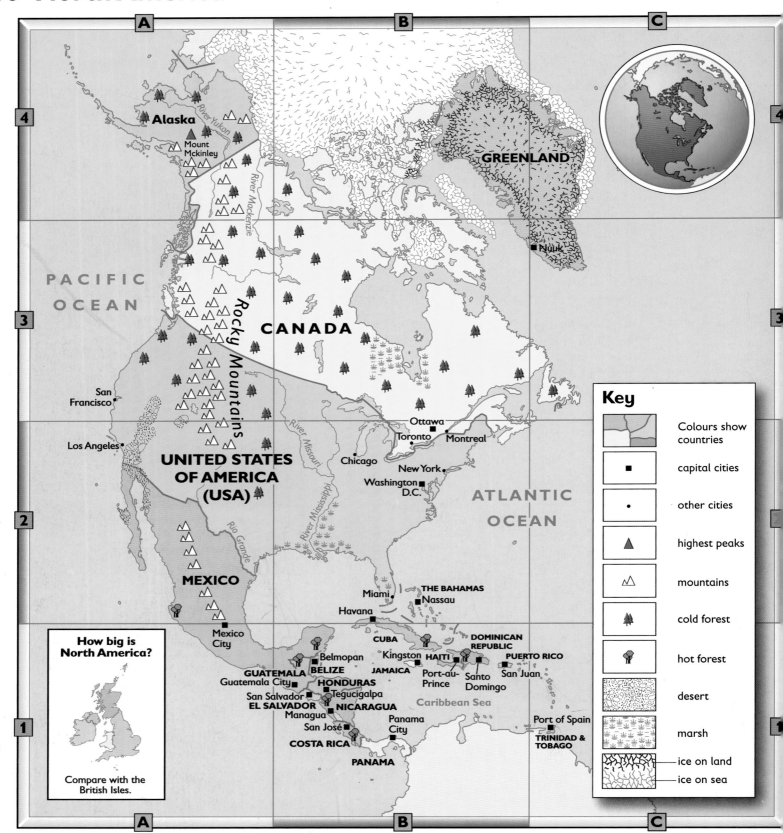

PACIFIC
OCEAN

Alaska

Mount
Mckinley

River Yukon

River Mackenzie

Rocky Mountains

CANADA

GREENLAND

Nuuk

San
Francisco

Los Angeles

River Missouri

**UNITED STATES
OF AMERICA
(USA)**

Chicago

River Mississippi

Rio Grande

Ottawa
Toronto
Montreal

New York

Washington
D.C.

ATLANTIC
OCEAN

MEXICO

Miami

Havana

THE BAHAMAS
Nassau

Mexico
City

CUBA

Kingston

**DOMINICAN
REPUBLIC**

JAMAICA

HAITI

Port-au-
Prince

Santo
Domingo

PUERTO RICO
San Juan

Belmopan
BELIZE

GUATEMALA
Guatemala City

HONDURAS

San Salvador   Tegucigalpa
EL SALVADOR

Managua

NICARAGUA

San José

Panama
City

Caribbean Sea

Port of Spain

**TRINIDAD &
TOBAGO**

COSTA RICA

PANAMA

How big is
North America?

Compare with the
British Isles.

Key

	Colours show countries
■	capital cities
•	other cities
▲	highest peaks
⋀	mountains
🌲	cold forest
🌳	hot forest
	desert
	marsh
	ice on land
	ice on sea

Oblique Mercator Projection
© Oxford University Press

The United States of America is the richest country in the world.

The Statue of Liberty stands in New York harbour.

Mexico is famous for its spicy food.

School buses in the United States and Canada are painted yellow.

SCHOOL BUS

74

74

The president of the United States lives in the White House.

The capital of the United States is Washington D.C. Can you find it on the map?

40 South America

A | B | C

4

Caracas

VENEZUELA

Bogota
Georgetown
Paramaribo
Cayenne

COLOMBIA
GUYANA **SURINAME**
FRENCH GUIANA

Quito

ECUADOR

Galapagos
Islands

River Amazon

PACIFIC

OCEAN

3

BRAZIL

PERU

Lima

BOLIVIA

Brasilia

La Paz

Atacama Desert

PARAGUAY

São Paulo
Rio de Janeiro

Asuncion

River Parana

ATLANTIC

OCEAN

2

Mount
Aconcagua

URUGUAY

Santiago
Buenos Aires
Montevideo

ARGENTINA

Key

	Colours show countries
■	capital cities
•	other cities
▲	highest peaks
⌂	mountains
	savannah
	hot forest
	desert
	marsh

How big is South America?

Compare with the British Isles.

1

A | B | C

Oblique Mercator Projection
© Oxford University Press

In the Amazon rainforest it is very hot and it rains every day. Trees in the forest are being cut down.

Carnaval in Brazil is a street party that lasts for five days.

These giant tortoises live in the Galapagos Islands.

The Amazon rainforest has very many plants, animals and insects.

Angel Falls in Venezuela is the world's highest waterfall.

The Atacama Desert is the driest place in the world. Can you find it on the map?

42 Africa

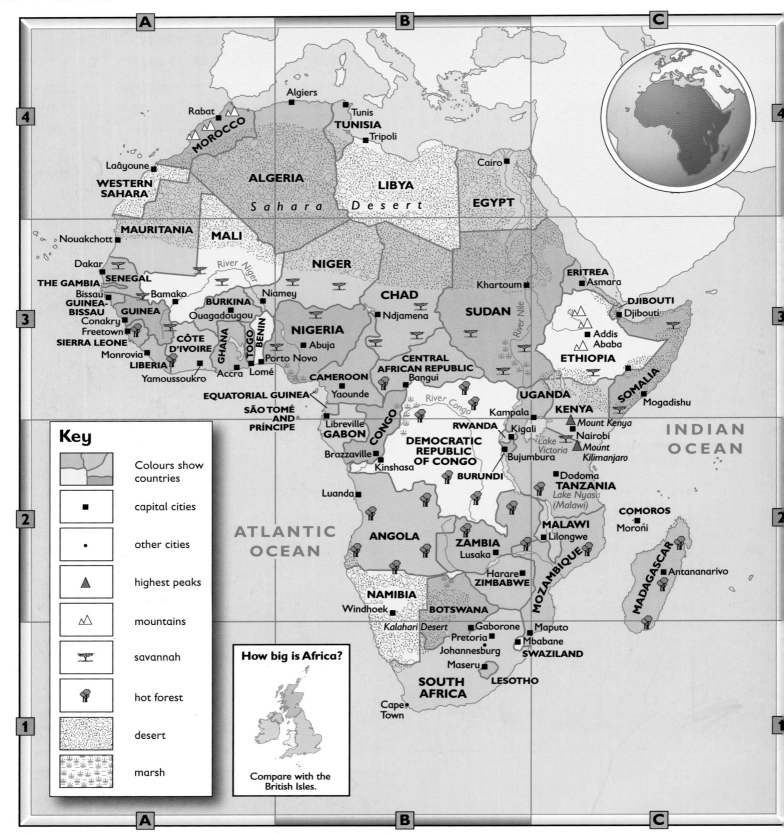

A B C

4 3 2 1

Algiers
Rabat
MOROCCO
Tunis
TUNISIA
Tripoli
Laâyoune
WESTERN SAHARA
ALGERIA
LIBYA
Cairo
EGYPT
Sahara Desert

MAURITANIA
Nouakchott
Dakar
SENEGAL
MALI
River Niger
NIGER
THE GAMBIA
Bissau
Bamako
GUINEA-BISSAU
GUINEA
Conakry
Freetown
SIERRA LEONE
Monrovia
LIBERIA
Yamoussoukro
CÔTE D'IVOIRE
GHANA
Accra
TOGO
BENIN
Lomé
Porto Novo
BURKINA
Ouagadougou
Niamey
NIGERIA
Abuja
Khartoum
CHAD
Ndjamena
SUDAN
River Nile
ERITREA
Asmara
DJIBOUTI
Djibouti
Addis Ababa
ETHIOPIA
CENTRAL AFRICAN REPUBLIC
Bangui
CAMEROON
Yaounde
EQUATORIAL GUINEA
SÃO TOMÉ AND PRÍNCIPE
Libreville
GABON
CONGO
Brazzaville
Kinshasa
River Congo
DEMOCRATIC REPUBLIC OF CONGO
RWANDA
Kigali
BURUNDI
Bujumbura
UGANDA
Kampala
KENYA
Mount Kenya
Nairobi
Mount Kilimanjaro
Lake Victoria
SOMALIA
Mogadishu
Luanda
Dodoma
TANZANIA
Lake Nyasa (Malawi)
COMOROS
Moroni
ANGOLA
ZAMBIA
Lusaka
MALAWI
Lilongwe
Harare
ZIMBABWE
MOZAMBIQUE
MADAGASCAR
Antananarivo
NAMIBIA
Windhoek
BOTSWANA
Kalahari Desert
Gaborone
Maputo
Pretoria
Mbabane
Johannesburg
SWAZILAND
Maseru
LESOTHO
SOUTH AFRICA
Cape Town

ATLANTIC OCEAN
INDIAN OCEAN

Key

	Colours show countries
■	capital cities
•	other cities
▲	highest peaks
⌂	mountains
	savannah
	hot forest
	desert
	marsh

How big is Africa?

Compare with the British Isles.

Zenithal Equal Area Projection
© Oxford University Press

Africa is a continent with many different countries and many different environments.

The pyramids are where ancient Egyptians buried their dead kings.

The savannah is dry. These wildebeest and zebra are thirsty.

Going shopping on market day in Mali.

These girls are getting water from the well.

The Sahara Desert is the largest desert in the world. Can you find it on the map?

44 Oceania

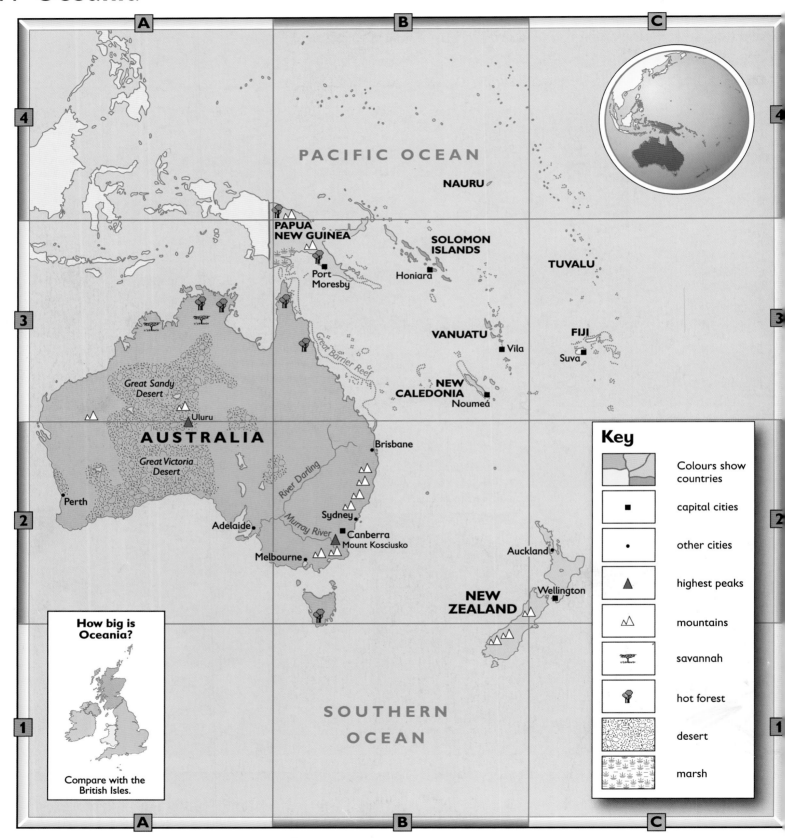

Australia is on the other side of the Earth to the British Isles. When it is winter in Britain, it is summer in Australia.

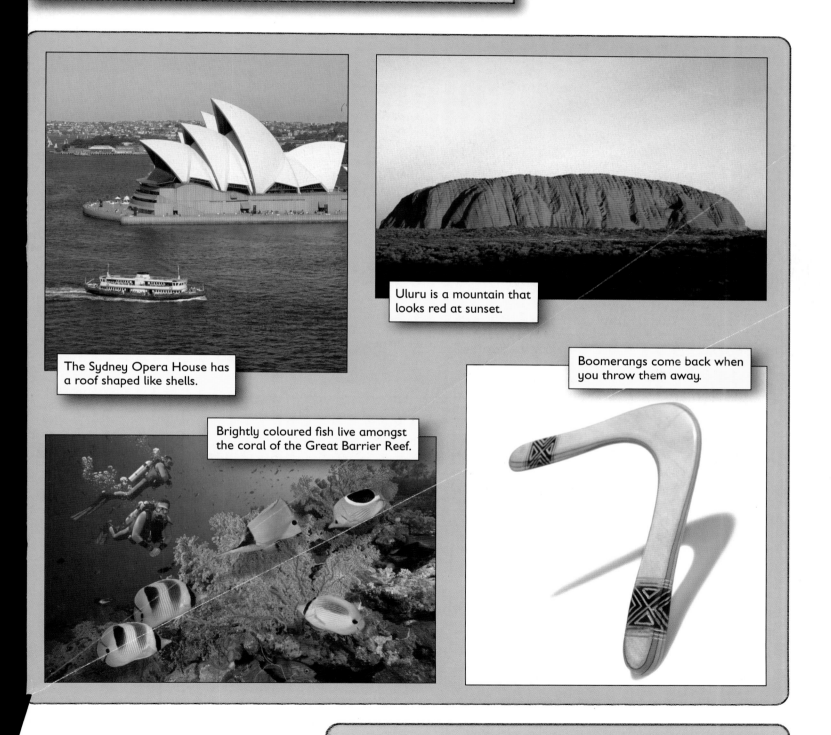

Uluru is a mountain that looks red at sunset.

The Sydney Opera House has a roof shaped like shells.

Boomerangs come back when you throw them away.

Brightly coloured fish live amongst the coral of the Great Barrier Reef.

There are many islands in Oceania. Can you name some of them?

46 Antarctica

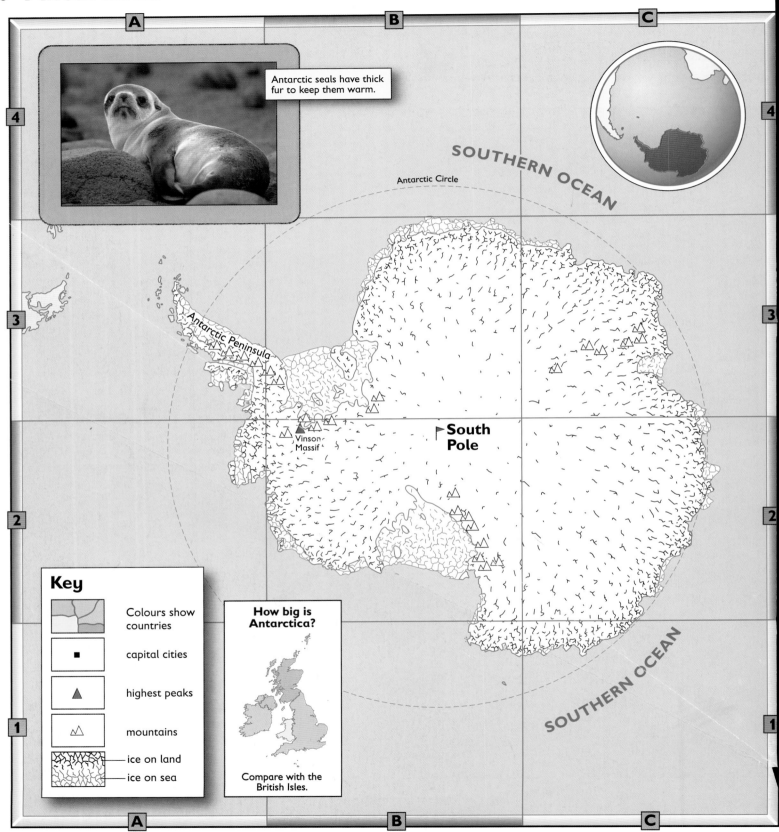

Antarctic seals have thick fur to keep them warm.

SOUTHERN OCEAN

Antarctic Circle

Antarctic Peninsula

Vinson Massif

South Pole

SOUTHERN OCEAN

Key

Colours show countries

■ capital cities

▲ highest peaks

△ mountains

ice on land

ice on sea

How big is Antarctica?

Compare with the British Isles.

Zenithal Equidistant Projection
© Oxford University Press

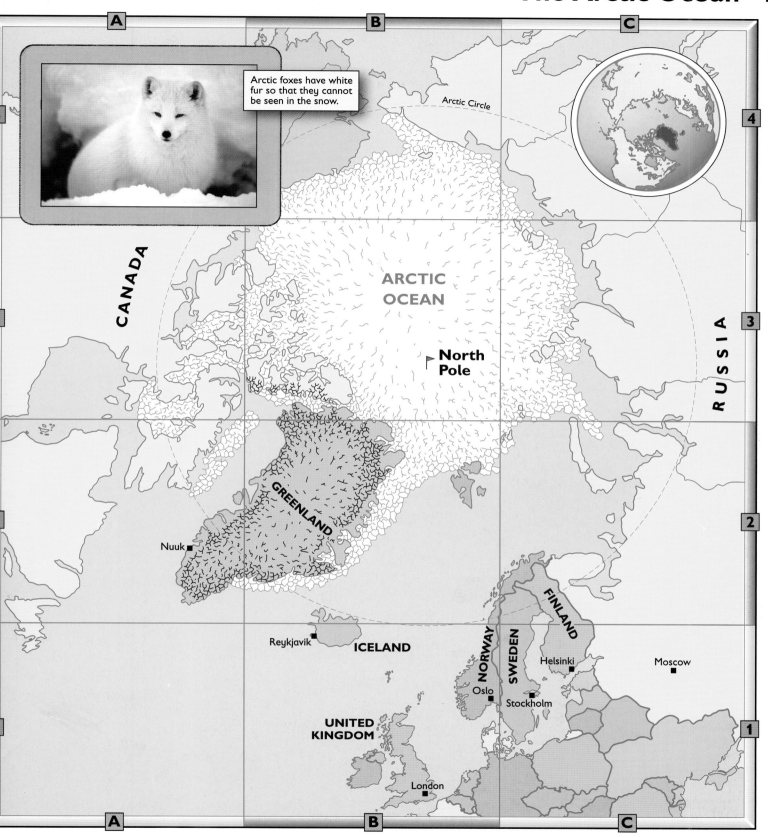

A   B   C

Arctic foxes have white fur so that they cannot be seen in the snow.

Arctic Circle

CANADA

ARCTIC
OCEAN

⌐ **North
Pole**

RUSSIA

GREENLAND

Nuuk ■

Reykjavik ■   **ICELAND**

FINLAND

NORWAY SWEDEN

Helsinki ■   Moscow ■

Oslo ■
Stockholm ■

**UNITED
KINGDOM**

London ■

A   B   C

4

3

2

1

Oxford University Press

A list of some of the most important places in this atlas.

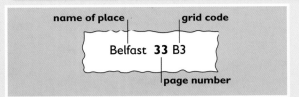

name of place   grid code

Belfast **33** B3

page number

World Flags

  Afghanistan

Albania

Algeria

Andorra

Angola

Antigua and Barbuda

Argentina

Armenia

Australia

Austria

Azerbaijan

Bahamas

Bahrain

Bangladesh

Barbados

Belarus

Belgium

Belize

Benin

Bhutan

Bolivia

Bosnia-Herzegovina

Botswana

Brazil

Brunei

Bulgaria

Burkina

Burundi

Cambodia

Cameroon

Canada

Cape Verde

Central African Republic

Chad

Chile

China

Colombia

Comoros

Congo

Congo, Dem. Rep.

Costa Rica

Côte d'Ivoire

Croatia

Cuba

Cyprus

Czech Republic

Denmark

Djibouti

Dominica

Dominican Republic

East Timor

Ecuador

Egypt

El Salvador

Equatorial Guinea

Eritrea

Estonia

Ethiopia

Fiji

Finland

France

French Guiana

Gabon

Gambia

Georgia

Germany

Ghana

Greece

Greenland

Grenada

Guatemala

Guinea

Guinea-Bissau

Guyana

Haiti

Honduras

Hungary

Iceland

India

Indonesia

Iran

Iraq

Ireland

Israel

Italy

Jamaica

Japan

Jordan

Kazakhstan

Kenya

Kiribati

Kuwait

Kyrgyzstan

Laos

Latvia

Lebanon

Lesotho

Liberia